BASICALLY CANNABIS

Rev.Russell Britton
Copyright © 2020
All rights reserved.
ISBN:amazon/kindle

DEDICATION

 I want to dedicate this book to everyone that has stood up for this miraculous plant through its imprisonment. Special thanks to all the researchers that shared their knowledge so I could learn and teach others.Extra special thank you to all my great friends and family that gave me support even when my crusade seemed silly... Thank you god for giving me the opportunities and courage to achieve all my past and future accomplishments.

INTRODUCTION

I have constructed this hand book to explain the basics of cannabis and how to use it every day utilizing consumption. While it is not a cure all as some would like you to think, it does have numerous amazing medicinal properties.

I'll explain why I believe cannabis was used religiously and how to use it in everyday cooking as well as a bit about dosage,terpenes,farming,soil,decarbing,and much more. The why's and how-to's will be explained along with a lot of great recipes.

.

I have many hobbies besides preaching about cannabis that include animals, nature, prospecting, inventing, rock hounding, old cars and I would have to say being a Lichtenberg Pyrography artist is my favorite. See my page **Lightningstruck@facebook** I also have a page called potluck where you can find all kinds of interesting things.

chapter 1: overview

I know you're going to love my favorite

cannabutter home style recipes, but you can also use your cannabutter in any recipe you choose. The main thing to keep in mind is amount per serving per person. If your recipe calls for a whole cup of butter, that does not mean it has to be all cannabutter and of course, should not be. I advise much less especially if it's potent THC butter. You can always eat smaller portions, but if you like good food like I do

then that's just not going to happen. You should also consider taste, cannabis is not all that good tasting alone or in strong doses, but it all depends on personal taste, spices and food used. For instance, I think cannabutter marinates with chicken and turkey better than the historic "special brownies; but it's distasteful on bread or in coffee. It isn't bad in a light tea and I find it compliments some juices if not overdone.

Moderation is key. You should add a little to this and a little to that throughout your day. Cannabis is not just for cannabutter. You can ingest cannabis in many ways, and some will benefit you in ways the others won't. Now I will talk a bit about that, I'm not going to go into detail but enough so you understand the basics..

The plant is meant to be used as a whole, From the roots up and again you will receive different benefits from different parts of the plant depending how it is used and processed.
The roots are great for balms, lotions, conditioner and salves. It can also be boiled down for tea but make sure to wash it thoroughly.
The stalk can be used to make all kinds of things,clothes,wood,plastic,biofuel,ect… over 25000 products can be made from hemp stalk although there are different kinds of hemp also... the most common is grown for cbd but there is cbg, grain and fiber also.
 The leaves make great tea or butter and can be a garnish.
 Of course, it can also be used like any other part of the plant as previously described. And of course, the flower itself is great in any form but I love to keep some decarbed and groundup in a

shaker for a quick sprinkle here and
there.
Sprouts are full of nutrition and have a
great nutty flavor.
Hemp seeds and hemp hearts are a
phenomenal source of nutrition also and
considered one of the planet's
superfoods.

chapter 2: religion

I believe Jesus himself utilized this
amazing plant for religious and medicinal
purposes and here are a few reasons I

came to this conclusion.In Exodus 30:22-36, God gives the ancient Israelite's a recipe for making holy anointing oil.Most of the ingredients are known, but there's one that has been hard to decipher, "kaneh-bosm."Some say that this describes a plant called calamus, others like me believe its cannabis but they could also both mean the same thing.cannabis. It's also believed that Jewish people probably used cannabis to make their anointing oil. That's precisely the era in which Jesus grew up so it's easy to assume that he knew about and used the plant.

He was also known as Jesus Christ. You may think that Christ was his last name but it's really a religious title meaning "anointed one". More than likely the anointing oil used had cannabis in it.His healing powers also tell the tale. There are many

stories of him helping those who were blind or had eye problems. And we now know cannabis is great at treating glaucoma. Epilepsy was often described as a demon possession and the new testament tells stories where

Jesus"cast out devils." I believe these devils were epilepsy that he cured with cannabis.

I have faith he used cannabis in several ways to help with many things. Some say he used it in incense to help with schizophrenia, in ointments and salves for rashes, skin diseases, joint pain,in food to help with digestive problems and bowel pains.

All this sure does sound all too familiar to be a coincidence.Now reading off Exodus 3:1-17 describing Moses's spiritual experience on top of Mt. Sinai."That's where he saw the angel of the Lord. I believe that the bush Moses burned was cannabis and that's what caused his visions. I'm not saying he didn't see god, just that he had help from nature and that's why it's needed for true holy sacrament.And of course Genesis 1:12 kjv Describes God's making of the earth. "I have given you every herb bearing seed which is upon the face of all the earth," and "And God saw everything that he had made, and, behold, it was very good.These are just some of the things that have led me to believe that cannabis was meant as a religious sacrament and has more than just amazing medicinal values. Feel free to do your own research.

chapter 3: terpenes

Terpenes have a lot to do with your cannabis also since they will affect the smell and taste of the flower.
terpenes are the oils that give cannabis its smell and flavor. It also has a variety of amazing benefits you need to know about.It is the smell that fills the air when you open a jar of flower or pinch a bud, terpenes are the key to producing the unique odor and delicious flavor that we adore in cannabis. Terpenes are a combination of carbon and hydrogen which is naturally created by plants to attract insects that will benefit the plant, protect, pollinate and repel pests and

animals from the plant. In cannabis plants, terpenes form in the trichomes (tiny hairs). Since cannabis plants are wind pollinated,they primarily produce terpenes to protect themselves from plant-eating animals.With well over 100 different terpenes, the smells (nose) in each strain directly relate to the effects felt.

Choosing the right strain is the first step in cannabis consumption no matter if it's hemp or if it has thc,here are some examples and benefits.
Caryophyllene. A spicy smell, providing medical value for ulcers, arthritis, and gastrointestinal problems.

Limonene. This citrus-smelling terpene offers anti-fungal, anti-bacterial, and anti-inflammatory properties, and it can also help with depression and heartburn.

Linalool. Medicinal value includes relief of depression and anxiety, and the terpene smells sweet like flowers.

Myrcene offers an earthy smell and is good for relieving muscle tension, insomnia, and chronic pain.

chapter 4: decarboxylation

you are going to hear about decarbing your flower though it's not something you need to do with hemp but if your wanting the effects from the thc is detrimental.i do believe consuming the plant in full spectrum(raw) is better for us since were not destroying or changing the cannabinoids prior to consumption.with over a hundred,most we know nothing about it's easy to see why i believe this theory.

If you do want to decarb your flower here are the instructions.
Preheat your oven to 200° F.Break up cannabis buds by hand until they are in very small pieces. Place the pieces on a baking sheet in a single layer. Bake the cannabis for up to 45 minutes, mixing it

every 15 minutes to ensure even toasting.After the cannabis has turned a medium brown color and is dried, remove the baking sheet from the oven and give the cannabis time to cool. When handled, it should be crumbly. You can use a food processor to pulse the cannabis until it becomes coarsely ground or by hand like I like to do.

HINT
If you grow your own flower,make sure to harvest before the sun comes up or light comes on for the best tasting flower.

chapter 5: oils and syrup

CANNABIS OIL
There are a few ways to make the oil.
One method is with cooking oil and the
other uses alcohol,then you also have
a water based syrup for tea or any
water based recipes you want to try.
Whichever method you chose be sure
to decarb first for best results.
.
1. With OIL
With this method, you choose your
favorite carrier oil, such as butter, olive
or coconut oil.Choose buds, leaves,
and stems of a high-quality cannabis
plant. The quality of the cannabis that
will be used will dictate the quality of
the oil that will be produced.. The
amount of base oil used will depend
on how much plant you have, what
part of the plant, potency and how
potent you want your oil.
I like to use flower and coconut oil at a
rationing of one quart of oil to one half
ounce of flower but this is where the fun
begins and you get to play. Don't forget

different strains will have different
potency & amp; terpenes also so your
recipe may need adjustments.
Now that you have your base oil and have
decarbed your plant just place desired
amounts of both in a pan and simmer on
low for 2-3 hrs. then let cool to room
temperature. Strain using a cheesecloth or
mesh filter and your oil is ready to be
used.

 2. with ALCOHOL
Also known as the ethanol method, it is
another process that does not require
special skills or advanced equipment,
making it another good choice for
beginners thinking of how to make cbd oil.
Alcohol is preferred as an extracting agent
because it does not leave an unpleasant
taste or odor.Put it in a ceramic or glass
bowl. Cover it with alcohol and stir for
about 6 minutes. Use a wooden spoon to
extract the resin. Place a straining bag or
sieve to filter the solvent out of the
container.
 Squeeze as much extract as possible.
You can repeat the process if you think

that you can still extract more oil from weed that you are squeezing. In a double boiler, pour the oil that you have earlier extracted. Heat it until bubbles start to form. Wait until the alcohol evaporates but do not raise the temperature. Wait until it simmers in about thirty minutes while making sure that the flame is low. Once the alcohol evaporates completely, mix it. Transfer the concentrated oil in a storage bottle. Be sure to keep the lid tight to avoid damaging its quality and effectiveness.

SYRUP

Cannabis Syrup is used in recipes that oil can't be.

1 ounce decarbed hemp or thc cannabis
½ gallon water or reduce recipe as needed.

Mix both ingredients in a large pot without a lid and set on simmer/low heat. Let cook for at least an hour but I suggest two while stirring consistently..

Add more water as needed. You should end up with about a half-gallon of syrup when finished. Let cool and strain into a glass jar with a mesh filter or cheesecloth.

This will be a potent mix if cannabis is good quality so use sparingly. You can use the flower you strained out in other recipes so don't throw it away! It's great in most sauces among other things so put it in the fridge to keep fresh.Dosage: this will vary every batch and it's always better to start with a little but one teaspoon per serving/person would be a good starting point.

chapter 6: farming

So, you want to grow your own medicine but don't know how. Cannabis is a very hearty plant but not as easy as you may believe. Most people's first and biggest mistake is over watering. It's easy to do because you want your baby to grow up fast and healthy, but all

what you're doing is rotting its roots and killing it. I like to let my soil dry out quite a bit before watering again. You also want to start with good soil but nothing with time release nutrients, you want to control what nutrients to add and when or if you can "burn" your plant. If your soil is amended well enough you will not need to add anything but water, music and love. Yes, I said music. I have found my plants love music and it helps keep gophers, moles and other critters away.Let's talk a bit about amendments since it's pretty important to your success. If you are using soil from your yard, I would suggest you take several samples from all over the planting are,mix it up good and then send that off for testing.You also want to test your water and make sure not to use any water hooked up to a water softener that uses salt.Once you know what you have you can amend accordingly.your soil and water ph can cause severe problems if not kept between 5 and 7...this is very important and often overlooked by first time growers.

NUTRIENTS
Cannabis production requires up to 100-130 lb. of nitrogen/ acre, 45-70 lb. phosphorus /acre, and 35-80 lb. potash/acre to keep potassium levels in a medium to high range of 250 ppm. Hemp

requires good nitrogen fertilization, Phosphorus levels should be medium to high (40 ppm),sulfur good (5,000 ppm), and calcium not in excess (6,000 ppm). In addition to well aerated,loamy soils, hemp does best with organic matter greater than 3.5%. If your soil is within these guidelines you have a basic good soil. You can also just go to your local nursery and buy goods oil to start with. Though I still recommend amendments. Here is a basic recipe you will love.Amendments needed per yard. A yard will fill (40) five-gallon buckets.

15 lb. worm castings
5 lb. fish bone meal
5 lb. blood meal
1 lb. bat guano
1 lb. azomite

It may be beneficial to add dolomite lime to help with soil pH balance. This is just a base to start from to get started.there is a lot more that you can do that would benefit the plant from root enzymes to beneficial nematodes..

HINT
Unsulphured blackstrap molasses will

fatten buds and help sweeten their taste. I use a few tablespoons per gallon throughout the bloom cycle.

DRYING AND CURING

In order to get the best results from your cannabis it needs to be dried and cured correctly.You will want to hang your plants in a dark space with 60% humidity at 60 degrees for about ten days. The stems will snap,not bend when dry.. then you will want to store your harvest in mason jars or plastic totes for 30 days burping daily

for the first three weeks.. burping means
taking the lid off and tossing the product
around a bit for about five minutes in order
to prevent mold..

chapter 7:pest management

another crucial aspect of growing
cannabis..there are several ways
to tackle a bug problem but it's
best to keep from getting one to
begin with..

With cannabis being an agricultural crop,
the solutions to its cultivation problems lie

within traditional agriculture practices.
 A well-crafted IPM(INTEGRATED PEST MANAGEMENT) plan helps create a balanced ecosystem, provides alternatives to pesticide usage, saves money, establishes a safer work environment for employees and can enhance a cultivator's image. A balanced ecosystem keeps one species from overpopulating and doing damage to another species. But with pesticide usage, the balance is destroyed by killing both the pest and its natural predator, and unintentionally causing the pest to become resistant to the pesticide used. The chance of resistance increases within improper application. IPM only applies a pesticide at the right moment in a pest's life cycle, when the pesticide will be most effective.

A good ipm will be adopted by the climate or if you're growing indoors so again i'm just going to stick to some basics to help you get started..
praying mantis,assassin,bugs,lady bugs,green lace wings,and beneficial nematodes are welcome sights in your

garden.. while there are lots of enemies out there make sure to let these thrive...

You can also use essential oils but as stated above this could run the good guys away also neem and.peppermint oil being the most commonly used.

Now as far as chemical pesticides, if you must use any,make sure it's omri approved and never spray the flower,I don't care what the label says... better safe than sorry.. And of course let's not forget companion planting and again this will kind of depend on climate and soil so do your research...

there are lots of companion plants that will help you with not only pest control but weeds also..any mints,chamomile,dill,lavender,sunflowers ,yarrow,basil,coriander,and marigolds but marigolds should be planted in pots,not with the cannabis.not only will these benefit your plants they can also benefit you..

chapter 8:recipes

The part you have been reading for the
recipes i'm going to start with breakfast
and finish with desserts..you can use any
recipe you like and just add your
preferred dose of oil & syrup..

FRENCH TOAST

2-3 eggs
4-6 slices of bread
1/3 cup whipping cream or milk
1tbs cannabutter
1/3 cup butter
Combine both butters and mix together thoroughly and set aside. In a separate bowl whisk eggs and milk together. This can also be made with no yolks if you prefer. Add any spices of your choosing to the mixture. Cinnamon is good but I tend to prefer mine vanilla but there are a ton of flavors for you to play with here, have fun. don't forget to whisk it in good though.In a frying pan add a tbs or so of

your butter mixture and put flame on medium heat while using your spatula to spread the melting butter. (I love that smell). Now you want to quickly dip a slice of bread into the egg mixture and cover it completely in your mixture. Get to be fast or your bread will fall apart. Place in the pan and repeat the process till the pan is full. You will want to cook 2-5 minutes on each side adding butter as needed, usually when I flip so I can get both sides covered.Cooking time will vary with each stove, pan type, and how temp is adjusted so keep an eye on it.Once your toast is cooked you can plate and embellish as you wish. My favorite is whipped cream and strawberries or just good old-fashioned maple syrup. any way you choose is sure to be yummy.

BISCUITS AND GRAVY

I'm not going to force you to make
biscuits from scratch, just use your
favorite brand prepared
per package instructions.
1 lb. sausage of choice.(I prefer breakfast
sausage myself)
1/4 cup cold water
2 tbsp all-purpose flour
1 tsp cannabutter
1 tsp salt
1 tsp black pepper
1/2 cup milk
Were going to start by mixing the flour,
salt, pepper and cold water together to
make a
paste then
set aside.
In a medium frying pan on medium-
high heat, brown the sausage well and

crumble into desired
sizes. Go ahead and add the milk and
cannabutter. Wait until hot again
before adding paste and
whisk until desired thickness is achieved.
Remove from heat and serve over biscuits.

POTATO AND ONION

1 large potato
1 large onion
1 tsp cannabutter
3 tsp butter
Salt and pepper
Dice or slice your veggies into small
pieces or thin slices. In a large frying
pan mix both butters
with heat on medium low. Once butters
are melted add your potatoes, onions
and spices to taste.
Cover and let cook for about 20
minutes stirring every few minutes.
And of course, your welcome to
use whatever spices you enjoy.

LIVER AND ONIONS

1 lb. liver
1 large diced onion
1 tbsp cannabutter
2 tbsp butter/oil of choice
Salt and pepper
On medium heat add your butter/oils
to a large frying pan with a lid. Once
hot add your onions
and stir them up well. Once a bit
browned slide the onions to the side of
the pan and add your
liver. Be sure to leave room in the pan
to stir everything and prevent burning.
Additional butter/oil can be added.
Cook for 3-6 minutes on both sides.
Enjoy!

BACON MAC AND CHEESE

Now of course you can just use a box of
Kraft and substitute some regular butter for
some
cannabutter but that's not near as tasty.
For the real deal you're going to need:
1 box elbow mac
1 lb. shredded sharp cheddar cheese
1/4 lb. diced Velveeta
1 cup milk
1 lb. cooked bacon bits w/grease (optional)
1 tsp salt
1 tsp black pepper

In a medium pan on low heat add your
milk and bacon grease if you have it. if
not, just proceed
without it. Add your Velveeta and let that
melt in a bit. You can add your salt and
pepper while
you wait. Now toss your shredded
cheddar in there and melt it all about.

Once your all melted up
It should be a little soupy. Add the bacon
and let it marry a while while stirring to
keep from scorching. (do not cover)
Usually 45 minutes to an hour is good. Boil
your pasta during this time
and once both are ready mix well and salt\
pepper to taste. I like to cook this mixture
a few minutes on medium stirring
constantly but it's up to you. Either way it's
sure to be yummy!

CHICKEN AND DUMPLINGS

If you're feeling blah this is one meal
that will not only fill you up but also
get you feeling good.
1lb chicken chunks
1 onion
2 tsp cannabutter
1 cup flour
1 tsp baking powder
1 egg
1/3 cup milk
2 cubes chicken bouillon
1/2 gallon chicken broth or water (I like it
half and half)
2 tsp salt
2 tsp black pepper
Add 1 tsp cannabutter, the
onion and chicken in a
medium-large frying pan on
medium-high heat
and cook well (8-12 min), don't forget to
stir..
While that's cooking in a large bowl mix

the flour,egg,1 tsp salt,1 tsp pepper, baking soda, milk
and crumble up 1 of the bouillon cubes. I like to add some of the bacon bits, but again this is
optional. Set this mixture aside for later.
In a large pan on medium-high heat you can add the broth/water, remaining spices, and butter.
Once the water is boiling, using a spoon, finger drop nuggets of the flour batter into the broth.
Let cook for 5 minutes then add chicken and onions. Cook an additional 15-20 minutes to thicken and marry it all together and you're ready to chow down.

MEATLOAF

3-4lbs ground beef
1 diced onion of choice
1 diced bell pepper
1 tbsp cannabutter
1 tsp salt
1 tbsp black pepper
1 tbsp Italian seasoning
I lg clove minced garlic
1/4 cup bread crumbs
1 egg
1 can tomato paste
Preheat the oven to 350 degrees. In a medium frying pan on medium heat add cannabutter, onion, half of the garlic and pepper. Let cook for about 10 minutes stirring periodically. Take half out and set aside to cool. Now add tomato paste to the remaining half. Stirring constantly to marry the flavors for about another ten minutes. This is a very important step and I highly advise you to do

not skip. Set this aside after ten minutes.
Mix all remaining ingredients in a large
bowl except the paste mixture. Once it's
all mixed it can
be formed into a loaf. I like to make
mine a little more like a cake but it's
your loaf, form per
your taste. Once formed, place in a
baking pan that has water in it, then
smother loaf with paste mixture.
cover and bake 45-60 minutes
adding water if needed every 15
minutes. Best
served with mashed potatoes and sweet
corn.

SALISBURY STEAK

1 1/2 lb. lean ground beef
1 diced onion(optional)
1 diced bell pepper(optional)
1 tsp cannabutter
1 tsp salt
1 tsp black pepper
1/2 cup breadcrumbs
1 batch of my special gravy made with 1/2 lb. meat.

This is a great recipe to add a tsp of that wet flower I told you to save to. In a large frying pan on medium heat caramelize the onion and pepper with the cannabutter then add the gravy and let simmer while the remaining ingredients are mixed together in a large bowl.Once mixed it can be shaped into thin patties and sprinkled with salt and pepper and added to the gravy.
Cook on low-medium heat for 45-60 minutes.

MEAT CAKE

This is a manly meal and is very

versatile because you can use almost any meat and veggie combination and is a tasty way to use up those leftovers. I'm going to give you my favorite combination to explain the recipe but feel free to play. Let's get started by getting our ingredients together.

1/4-1/2 lb. of whatever meats you choose. I'm going to use some leftover ham as an example.

1 cup onion or veggie of choice (optional)

1/2 cup cheddar cheese (optional)

3 whole eggs

1/4 cup pancake batter

1 tsp cannabutter

1 tsp salt

1 tsp black pepper

In a large frying pan on low-medium heat add your meat, veggie and cannabutter. Cooking time will vary by taste and meat/veggie being used so you will have to use your own and judgement/experience. Leftovers simply need heating while raw foods will take adequate time to

cook prior to the next step.
Now while you're waiting for that to cook
go ahead and whisk the eggs, salt,
pepper and pancake
Mix in a bowl for several minutes until
you don't see any more lumps and then
set aside. Once your Meat and veggies
are cooked to taste turn the stove up to
medium and mix your egg
batter in. Mix together quickly then
stop and let cook 2-3 minutes until the
cake can be flipped
over. Add cheese to top and cover. let
cook for 2-5 minutes and serve hot. This is
also great with sausage and drizzled with
syrup instead of cheese, steak strips with
bell
peppers and mozzarella cheese, bacon
and potatoes, the list is endless. enjoy
playing!

STOVE TOP STUFFING SHEPARDS PIE

1 lb. ground beef
1 diced onion
1 box stove top stuffing (cornbread)
1 pack brown gravy mix

1 cup water
1/2 cup melted butter
1 tsp cannabutter
1 tsp salt
1 tsp black pepper
2 cups mashed potatoes
Mix the cannabutter, beef, salt,
pepper and onion in a large frying
pan and cook 5-7 minutes on
medium-high heat or to taste. Then
mix everything but potatoes
together and put in casserole
dish or baking pan. Now layer the
mashed potatoes over it all like a
blanket and bake at 350° for
20 minutes.

GRILLED CHEESE SANDWICH

This is an all-time favorite on a cold day.
4 slices bread
4 slices of cheese
1 tsp cannabutter

1 tbsp butter

Thoroughly mix butters together and coat one side of bread. Set bread in large frying pan butter
side down on medium-high heat and add a slice of cheese to each slice of bread. Let cook 2-3
min then marry two of your pieces to make two delicious grilled cheese sandwiches. Brown to
taste and enjoy with a bowl of your favorite soup.

CANDIED YAMS

1 can yams
1 cup brown sugar
1 cup butter
2 tbsp cannabutter (you can use less if you like)
4 cups mini marshmallows

Add butters to a large pan on medium heat and let melt. Then add brown sugar and mix thoroughly before adding yams and reducing heat to low-medium. Let cook 30 minutes turning
yams over after 15 minutes. Add marshmallows and cover 3-5
minutes. Let cool a bit before
serving, they will be hot but delicious! Save the juice, it's great poured over a sweet bread like
pumpkin or sweet potato and can be used in sweet potato pie. I hate waste and this juice has a lot
of medicine in it so feel welcome to play with it to see how else you like to use it.
p27
RED SAUCE(SPAGHETTI SAUCE)

This recipe can be used with chicken or beef
1lb ground beef or diced chicken
1 onion(diced)
1 bell pepper(diced)
1 clove garlic(ground)
1 tbsp cannabutter
1 tsp sugar

1 tsp sea salt
1 tsp garlic powder or minced
2 tsp black pepper optional
1 tbsp Italian seasoning
1 large can/jar favorite sauce
1 can paste
1 box pasta of choice
In a large pan add sauce and a
can of water on low heat. add
sugar and garlic. Stir periodically.
In a large frying pan mix ground beef or
chicken with cannabutter and add 1tsp
salt and pepper
cooking on medium heat till
browned/cooked thoroughly.now add the
paste and cook for 3 minutes while
constantly stirring,this will make a huge
difference in flavor then add onion and
pepper and cook 5 more
minutes or to taste (onion/ pepper texture).
 When
this is complete it can be added to sauce
you have been simmering along with the
rest of the salt,
pepper and Italian seasoning.
Cook on low stirring periodically for at least
2 hours then serve with cooked pasta of

your
choice.

ALFREDO SAUCE

1/4 cup whipping cream
2 eggs
1 diced onion(optional)
1 diced bell pepper(optional)
1 tsp cannabutter
1 tsp butter
1 tsp salt
1 tsp black pepper
1 cup parmesan or to taste

If you're not using onions or bell
peppers skip this step and add
the butter in with remaining
ingredients as instructed below.
In a frying pan on medium-high heat add
the butters onion and peppers and cook
about 5 minutes
or to your taste then set aside.
In a large pan on high heat bring
cream to boil then whip in remaining
ingredients then eggs last
continuing to whip for 3-5 minutes on
medium heat. Remove from heat and add
the onion and
pepper mix then let cool a bit before
serving with your favorite pasta. I myself
prefer Angel Hair.

GRAVY

I love a good gravy and it's even better
medicated. You can make any kind of
gravy like this
all you need is a bit of scraps/grease for
the flavor.
1/4 cup cold water
2 tbsp all-purpose flour
1 tsp cannabutter
1 tsp salt
1 tsp black pepper
1/2 cup trimming grease flavoring
(grease from cooking a meat) or milk
Start by mixing the flour, salt, pepper

and cold water together to make a
paste then set aside.
In a medium frying pan on medium heat
add whatever your trimming grease is or
milk and cannabutter. Wait until hot then
add paste and whisk until desired
thickness. Remove from
heat
and serve.
Please remember if you medicate your
gravy you may not want to medicate
anything else and
vice versa. You don't want to eat a
serving of canna yams with medi
mashed potatoes covered in
yet again medicated gravy. It's very easy
to overdo consuming it. you won't know
until it is too
late, and you find you slept the day away.

GARLIC BUTTER

There are very few ways cannabutter
and bread go well together, this is
one of them. 1 stick sweet cream
butter
1 tsp cannabutter
1 large clove fresh ground butter
Now just mix it all up really well and use it
at will.

SWEET TEA

5 tea bags
1/4 cup Special Syrup
1 cup sugar
1-gallon water
In a small pan add a few cups of the water on high heat. Once boiling add tea bags. Cook 2-3 minutes stirring gently so you don't break the bags open. Turn off heat and remove tea bags. Add syrup and sugar and mix thoroughly before adding to remaining water and put in the fridge to chill.you can also add a teaspoon over your coffee grounds before you perk it for a good morning treat..

I know there aren't a lot of recipes here but my goal was to give you an idea of how it all works and how it can be utilized.you can use the butter or syrup in almost any recipes so please feel free to play.

chapter 9: cannabinoids explained

Now I'm going to try and explain this as simply as possible but it's just not a real simple answer.

Cannabinoids are chemical compounds that activate cannabinoid receptors, spread throughout the body of all vertebrates. Cannabinoid receptor activation interacts with neurotransmitters, which have a beneficial effect on our endocannabinoid system. Cannabinoids can be divided into three groups:

Phytocannabinoids (plant-based cannabinoids that are found in hemp and some other plants)
Endocannabinoids (cannabinoids produced in our bodies)

Synthetic cannabinoids (laboratory-produced cannabinoids)

Cannabis or hemp plants produce over 400 chemical compounds throughout its life cycle. More than 140 of that chemical (terpenophenolic) compounds are cannabinoids, found in trichomes. By discovering the therapeutic potential of cannabis, this number is only increasing with numerous studies. Cannabinoids are usually obtained from cannabis or hemp, but they could also be found in other cannabinoid plants.

Delta-9-tetrahydrocannabinol

THC in most commonly found cannabinoid in cannabis.THC is one of few psychoactive cannabinoids that bind to CB1 & CB2 cannabinoid receptors in the body, and is one of the main reasons that cannabis (except industrial hemp) is illegal in the majority of the world. Even though that THC is mostly abused for the recreational purpose, it can give us many beneficial effects when used correctly:
Reduces inflammation,
eases chronic pain,

reduces risk of heart disease,
inhibits macular degeneration and loss of
vision,
helps to treat symptoms in Parkinson's
disease,
increases appetite,
can slow down the progress of AIDS,
encourages the development of
neuroplasticity,
inhibits symptoms of post-traumatic stress
disorder,etc..

Cannabidiol CBD
CBD is considered the second most
researched cannabinoid in
cannabis.Cannabidiol (CBD) is non-
psychoactive cannabinoid that doesn't
get you high,but it does give us a wide
variety of benefits to maintain and
improve our health:
Reduces frequency of epileptic seizures,
eases chronic pain,
inhibits symptoms of psoriasis,
reduces risk of heart disease,
eases anxiety and paranoia,

stimulates the formation of new, healthy cells,
reduces risk of cancer,
contributes to the treatment of addiction,
prevents the formation of autoimmune diseases,
eliminates adverse effects of THC,
it has anti-inflammatory properties,etc.

Cannabigerol CBG the very first cannabinoid that all cannabinoids evolved from. According to studies, Cannabigerol is known to be the only cannabinoid with the ability to stimulate the growth of new brain cells. CBG is non-psychoactive cannabinoid and can have a beneficial effect on our body:
Acts as an antidepressant,
balances our well-being,
reduces pain,
it has antibiotic properties,
prevents redness of the skin,
inhibits tumor formation,
induces bone growth,etc.

Cannabinol CBN
Tetrahydrocannabinolic acid (THCA) is
transformed into a non-psychoactive CBN
cannabinoid by ageing and oxidation:
Cannabinol also provides many
beneficial effects: Stimulates appetite,
controls the further
development of the
lung tumor (Lewis
carcinoma), controls
the formation of
cancer cells,
inhibits symptoms of Amyotrophic lateral
sclerosis,
it has anti-epileptic properties,
works as a sedative,
it can potentiate some of the THC effects,
successfully fights Meticillin-resistant
bacteria (MRSA),etc.

Cannabichromene CBC
CBC is non-psychoactive and is the third

most common cannabinoid found in cannabis or hemp. In some cannabis strains, it can even exceed the cannabidiol (CBD) content. When CBC is used in combination with THC, its ability to relieve inflammation increases significantly. CBC predominantly interacts on TRPV1 and TRPA1 receptors and has many properties that can have a positive effect on our health:
Works as an antidepressant, stimulates neurogenesis, mitigates fungal inflammation
it has anti-inflammatory properties, increases analgesic effect in medical cannabis,
in combination with other cannabinoids (THC, CBD in CBG), it can effectively deal with tumors and their emergence,etc.

Tetrahydrocannabivarin THCV
THCV is a derivative of THC and it has similar chemical structure. It is said that in small quantities THC acts as a THC

cannabinoid antagonist (it reduces its effects), but in bigger quantities acts as a THC cannabinoid agonist (it encourages its effects). Because
there is a lack of studies, it is hard to say if THCV is a psychoactive or non-psychoactive cannabinoid.
It has the ability to regulate blood sugar level,
stimulates bone growth,
reduces appetite,
it has neuroprotective properties,
it has anti-epileptic properties,
reduces the possibility of panic attacks,
etc.

Cannabidivarin CBDV

Cannabidivarin is CBD homologue and shares a similar chemical structure. CBDV is found in small quantities in hemp and is a non-psychoactive cannabinoid. Even though there is a lack of studies, it is known that cannabidivarin has similar therapeutic properties as cannabidiol (CBD), but with certainty, we can only assert that CBDV helps to reduce nausea and prevent epileptic seizures.

chapter 10: lagniappe

I'm just going to ramble a bit here about a few things..now that hemp is federally legal and most states allow farming we are seeing lots of products coming out so i want you to understand there are

dangers. You see,cannabis is a bioaccumulator. It will sponge up bad stuff from the soil like pesticides,heavy metals, and even radiation which is one of the ways it can help our planet.make sure if you grow your own that your allowed to do so or i'm not responsible but also get the soil tested if not purchased soil,also if your buying a
consumable product make sure it has passed testing for these issues.there are fake products you should be aware of "caveat emptor"... make sure what your purchasing is what you want..
hemp oil is not cbd oil and cbd oil is not cbg oil..

ABOUT THE AUTHOR

I kinda already gave you my bio but i did not tell you why i have been learning and preaching about this plant the past 4 years..about 8 yrs ago we lost our 12 year little girl to a really rare disease called pkan,the loss was devastating and it was a long horrid ordeal i wouldn't wish on the devil. to lose a child is hard enough,to lose a child that was in excruciating pain and in the end had to starve to death and nothing we could do about it..about 4years later i learned cannabis may have helped,it would not of saved ashley,but it may of made her much more comfortable..so you see,this is a passion,i believe we need these cannabinoids in our bodies to help keep us and our children healthy.

Made in the USA
Monee, IL
15 February 2021